The Story of

CHOCOLATE

by Gloria Koster

PEBBLE
a capstone imprint

Published by Pebble, an imprint of Capstone
1710 Roe Crest Drive, North Mankato, Minnesota 56003
capstonepub.com

Library of Congress Cataloging-in-Publication Data
Names: Koster, Gloria, author.
Title: The story of chocolate / by Gloria Koster.
Description: North Mankato, Minnesota : Pebble, an imprint of
Capstone, [2024] | Series: Stories of everyday things | Includes
bibliographical references and index. | Audience: Ages 5-8
Audience: Grades K-1
Summary: "Chocolate is a favorite treat for many people,
but where does it come from? What is it made from? How is it turned
into the sweet treats people love? Tackle your hunger for knowledge
with this informative book on chocolate."—Provided by publisher.
Identifiers: LCCN 2023027857 (print) | LCCN 2023027858 (ebook)
| ISBN 9780756577469 (hardcover) | ISBN 9780756577636
(paperback) | ISBN 9780756577520 (pdf) | ISBN 9780756577650
(kindle edition) | ISBN 9780756577643 (epub)
Subjects: LCSH: Chocolate—History—Juvenile literature.
Classification: LCC TX767.C5 K67 2024 (print) | LCC TX767.C5
(ebook) | DDC 641.3/374—dc23/eng/20230623
LC record available at https://lccn.loc.gov/2023027857
LC ebook record available at https://lccn.loc.gov/2023027858

Editorial Credits
Editor: Alison Deering; Designer: Jaime Willems; Media Researcher:
Rebekah Hubstenberger; Production Specialist: Whitney Schaefer

Image Credits
Alamy: Cavan Images, 25; Associated Press: Paul Ross/VWPics,
9; Getty Images: gustavo ramirez, 15, Hulton Archive, 11,
iStock/anamariategzes, 28, iStock/DavorLovincic, 10, iStock/
joshuaraineyphotography, 19, iStock/Say-Cheese, 20, SolStock,
Back Cover, 21, sutiporn somnam, 22, ZU_09, 13; Shutterstock:
And-One, Cover (top right), BestForBest, 7, dassy100, 1, Elena Uve,
Cover (top left, middle left, bottom right), Farion_O, Cover (bottom
left), Gabrielle Prosser, 4, JLco Julia Amaral, 27, Keith Homan, 23, Lais
Monteiro, Cover (middle), Miro Vrlik Photography, 16, Nikola Bilic, 17,
Photoongraphy, 6, PixieMe, 5; The Metropolitan Museum of Art: Gift
of George O. May, 1943, 12

Design Elements
Shutterstock: Luria, Pooretat moonsana

Printed and bound in China. PO 5593

Table of Contents

What Is Chocolate? 4

The First Chocolate..8

Great Inventions 14

From Farm to Factory..18

Chocolate Today.. 22

    Hot Chocolate Stirrers............................. 28

    Glossary...30

    Read More 31

    Internet Sites.. 31

    Index 32

    About the Author.....................................32

Words in bold appear in the glossary.

What Is Chocolate?

What is your favorite sweet treat? Maybe you like cookies. Or maybe you love cake and ice cream. No matter what, chocolate is a popular choice. But where does it come from?

Cacao flowers grow on trees.

All chocolate comes from **cacao** beans. They grow on cacao trees in rain forests. Pink and white flowers grow on the trunks and branches. One tree can grow 6,000 flowers in a year! Only three to 10 percent will become cacao **pods**.

Cacao pods change color as they ripen.

Pods start out green. They ripen in five to six months. They turn yellow, red, or orange. A ripe pod is 8 to 14 inches (20 to 36 centimeters) long. It is shaped like a football.

Pods are very hard on the outside. But look inside! There are 20 to 60 seeds. These are called beans. They may not look like much. But they are the start of all the chocolate we eat. So who first discovered them?

The First Chocolate

Chocolate is not new. It was first discovered thousands of years ago in Mexico and Central America. The **Olmec** people were the first to crack open cacao pods.

The **Maya** later planted the beans. They used them to trade with the **Aztecs**. Aztec land was very dry. They could not plant their own beans.

Maya women make hot chocolate.

Cacao beans are ground by hand.

The Maya and Aztecs both crushed the beans. Then they added water. This was the first chocolate. It was liquid. But it was not like today's sweet chocolate drinks. It was **bitter**. People added spices to make it taste better.

The Maya believed cacao beans were a gift from the gods. People drank chocolate at daily events. The Aztecs served it only to the rich. Their ruler drank it from a golden cup. He drank 50 cups a day!

Chocolate was a favorite drink of the Aztec emperor.

In the 1500s, Spanish explorers learned about cacao beans. They sent them back to Spain. People there named the drink chocolatl. It was served hot. People added sugar. Delicious!

A chocolate pot

French royalty enjoyed chocolate.

In 1660, a Spanish princess married a French king. She brought chocolate with her to France. Soon it was popular in other countries.

Only rich people could afford chocolate back then. Friends met at chocolate houses. They drank from fancy bowls.

Great Inventions

New **inventions** changed chocolate. First came the steam engine. It was invented in the 1700s. This made it easier to grind beans. Chocolate became less expensive.

The chocolate press came in 1828. It separated the inside of the bean into two parts—fatty cocoa butter and dry cocoa mass. The mass was later crushed into cocoa powder.

Cocoa powder made a tastier drink. An Englishman named J.S. Fry thought cocoa butter could be used too. He combined melted cocoa butter, cocoa powder, and sugar. He poured the mixture into **molds**. Ta-da! Chocolate bars!

In Switzerland, Henri Nestlé invented powdered milk. His neighbor Daniel Peter added it to cocoa butter. He made the first milk chocolate.

Another Swiss inventor made chocolate even tastier. Rodolphe Lindt created a unique grinding system. It made chocolate smooth and creamy. Yum!

Milton S. Hershey started using **mass production** in the United States. His factory used machines to quickly turn out lots of chocolate kisses and candy bars. Today, the company makes more than 70 million Hershey's Kisses a day!

From Farm to Factory

There are many different types of chocolate to choose from. But each one starts the same way.

Ripe pods are cut from trees. The pods are split. The beans are removed. They are put in a dark place for about five days. Next they are dried in the sun. Then the beans are sent to a factory. It takes 400 beans to make 1 pound (0.45 kilogram) of chocolate!

The beans are cleaned. They are cooked at a high temperature. Outside shells are removed. The insides are called nibs. These are ground into a paste. The paste is pressed. Cocoa mass is separated from cocoa butter.

Cocao nibs roast in the sun.

Cocoa powder, cacao beans, and pieces of chocolate

For cocoa powder, the mass is ground again. Sugar is added. This powder will be used for baking and chocolate drinks.

For solid chocolate, cocoa butter is melted. Cocoa mass and sugar are added. Machines pour the mixture into molds.

Chocolate products are wrapped and packaged. Then they are shipped to stores.

People buy chocolate in every season. But it is extra popular during holidays. The most chocolate is sold during Easter. Shelves are filled with chocolate bunnies and chocolate eggs.

Chocolate Today

Chocolate farming is hard work. Farmers can't keep up with demand. Every year they lose crops. Sometimes trees don't get enough rain. This is because of **climate** change.

A farmer holds cacao pods.

The work is also dangerous. Farmers use sharp tools to split pods by hand. Some farms use chemicals to kill bugs. They can also be harmful to people. Organic farms do not use these. Read the label on your next chocolate bar. Does it say organic?

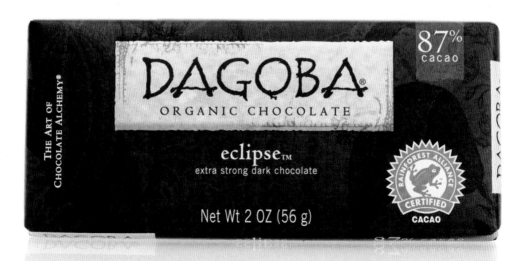

Most chocolate farms today are in West Africa. Many farmers do not make enough money. Children sometimes work alongside adults. Some countries do not have laws to protect these workers.

We can help farmers if we buy **fair trade** chocolate. Farmers are paid a fair price. These chocolate farms work to protect the **environment**.

A family sorts through cacao pods.

Each year people eat about 16 billion pounds (7.5 million tons) of chocolate! Not everyone can have chocolate. Some people have food allergies. Family pets should never have chocolate. It can make them sick.

Chocolate provides energy. It boosts our mood. Eating it makes us feel happy. Just don't overdo it!

Hot Chocolate Stirrers

Chocolate stirrers are a yummy way to enjoy a sweet treat. Try this fun activity with your friends and a grown-up.

What You Need:

- cooking oil or spray
- ice cube tray
- bag of chocolate chips*
- heatproof bowl
- spoon or spatula
- wooden popsicle sticks

*Choose your favorite chocolate. You can use milk chocolate, dark chocolate, or white chocolate.

What You Do:

1. Place an ice cube tray in the freezer for 10–15 minutes. Once chilled, take it out and lightly spray or wipe each section with cooking oil.

2. Pour chocolate chips into a heatproof bowl. Place the bowl in the microwave and heat for 30 seconds. Stir the chips and heat for another 20 seconds, then stir again. (If your chips still aren't melted, heat for longer, but check and stir them every 10–15 seconds.)

3. Pour melted chocolate into sections of the ice cube tray. Fill the sections 2/3 of the way to the top.

4. Add a popsicle stick to each section. Make sure the stick touches the bottom of the tray.

5. Place the ice cube tray in the refrigerator. Chill for 1 hour or until the chocolate cubes are solid.

6. Pop the stirrers from the tray and enjoy! You can dip one into a mug of warm milk for a yummy hot chocolate treat. You can also enjoy it as a chocolate lollipop!

Glossary

Aztec (AZ-tek)—Indigenous people who lived in Mexico before Spanish people settled there

climate (KLY-muht)—average weather of a place throughout the year

environment (in-VY-ruhn-muhnt)—all of the trees, plants, water, and dirt

fair trade (FAYR TRYD)—a way of buying and selling goods that allows farmers to be paid a fair price and have better working conditions

mass production (MASS pruh-DUHK-shuhn)—making goods in large amounts using machinery

Maya (MY-uh)—Indigenous people who live in southern Mexico and Central America

mold (MOHLD)—a form used to give food a decorative shape

Olmec (OHL-mek)—ancient people from the southern east coast of Mexico who lived there from about 1200 to 400 BCE

pod (POD)—a long case that holds the seeds of certain plants, such as peas

Read More

Cohen, Tziporah. *On the Corner of Chocolate Avenue: How Milton Hershey Brought Milk Chocolate to America.* New York: Clarion Books, 2022.

Grack, Rachel. *Cocoa Bean to Chocolate.* Minneapolis: Bellwether Media, Inc., 2020.

Hansen, Grace. *How Is Chocolate Made?* Minneapolis: Abdo Kids, 2018.

Internet Sites

Easy Science for Kids: Chocolate easyscienceforkids.com/best-melting-chocolate-video-for-kids/

Kiddle: History of Chocolate Facts for Kids kids.kiddle.co/History_of_chocolate

Official Kids Mag: Chocolate: A Sweet History officialkidsmag.com/2020/02/01/chocolate-a-sweet-history/

Index

allergies, 26
Aztecs, 8, 10–11

cacao
  beans, 5, 7, 8,
      10–11, 12,
      14, 18–19
  flowers, 5
  nibs, 19
  pods, 5, 6–7, 8,
      18, 22, 23, 25
  trees, 5, 18, 22
Central America, 8
chemicals, 23
chocolate houses,
    13

chocolatl, 12
climate change, 22
cocoa
  butter, 14–15, 16,
      19, 20
  mass, 14, 19, 20
  powder, 14–15, 20

factories, 17, 18
fair trade, 24
farming, 22, 23, 24
France, 13
Fry, J.S., 15

Hershey, Milton S.,
    17
holidays, 21

inventions, 14,
    16–17

Lindt, Rodolphe,
    16

Maya, 8, 10–11
Mexico, 8
molds, 15, 20

Nestlé, Henri, 16

Olmec, 8
organic farms, 23

Spain, 12
Switzerland, 16

West Africa, 24

About the Author

A public and a school librarian, Gloria Koster belongs to the Children's Book Committee of Bank Street College of Education. She enjoys both city and country life, dividing her time between Manhattan and the small town of Pound Ridge, New York. Gloria has three adult children and a bunch of energetic grandkids.